The Forgotten Love

The Forgotten Love

Poems of
Love & Longing

Taya Malakian
Gopalpreet

2017
GOLDEN DRAGONFLY PRESS

FIRST PRINT EDITION, February 2017
FIRST EBOOK EDITION, February 2017

Copyright © 2017 by Gopalpreet Taya Malakian.
All rights reserved.
Cover Photo by Wes Parrish.
Back Cover Photo by Kiera Haddock of Kiera Eve Photography

First published in the United States of America
by Golden Dragonfly Press, 2017.

No part of this document may be reproduced or transmitted in any form
or by any means, electronic or otherwise, without prior written permission
by the copyright owner.

www.goldendragonflypress.com

Dedicated to the Lovers
Who Remember

I write poems
about the simple things…
like love and longing
and the plain mystery that
our eyes choose not to see…

CONTENTS

About the Poems   xiii
Acknowledgements   xv

They Come Like Rain   1
The Forgotten Love   2
Do Not Wait to Pray   3
Waterfall   4
Suffering   5
Karma   6
The Poems of Desire   7
Let Me Remember   8
Beauty   9
Proof   10
Appreciation   11
Soften   13
Here I Am Again   14
Incense   15
Angel   16
Angels & Demons   17
Trust   18
Hide & Seek   19
Bless Them   20
Sinners & Saints   21
Nature   22
Sit   23
Gold   24
Courage   25
Sound   26
Diamond Eye   27
Union   28
Relax   29

Flawed Design	30
Madness	31
Snow	32
The Saints Do It Too	33
Bonsai	34
Sing	35
Ward of the Universe	36
Mara	37
Heaven.Hell	38
Forgetful	39
Lover	40
The Order of Things	41
Here	42
Little Moon	43
The Mirror	44
Your Rhythm	46
Worthy of Love	47
Summer	48
Please Show Me	49
Limitless Supply	50
Woman	51
The Chase	53
Hidden Things	54
The Cavern	55
Good Day	57
Diamonds	58
Waiting Room	59
Your True Name	60
Humans	61
Open	62
Our Storm	63
Huntress	64
Truth	65
The Reconcile	66
Wither	67

Special Someone	68
Dark	69
Moth	70
Shadow King	71
Terma	73
Man	74
Study	75
Love Unfulfilled	76
Old Love	77
Remember Me	78
Sister | Brother	79
One	81
Wick	82
Elements	83
Dream	84
Close	85
This World	86
Naked	88
Whenever Water is Near	89
Lost I	90
Lost II	91
Equinox	92
Poisons	93
The Queen Upon Her Throne	94
A Bottle to Hold Everything	95
Channeling Love	96
Your Breathing	97
Ghosts	98
Bonfire	99
Courtesan	100
Sky Dancer	102
Melt	103
I Want You	104
Longing	105
Season	106

Smolder	107
Like This	108
The Soul's Poem	109
Essence	110
If Anyone Was Watching	111
Thousand Steps to Spirit	112
Kindness	113
A Taste of This Love	114
About the Poet	115

About the Poems

These poems come from my experience exploring the depths as a yogini, an artist, a mother, a lover and a woman.

These poems come through in moments when I least expect or in times when I call for them to explain this world and its dramas. The Natural World, the Divine, the Universe inspires me to no end and I draw on the insights shared in nature or in meditation when writing. The poems return to me and find their way to others when they are needed most.

These poems are always here for you too, to share when you can't find the words to say what you mean or to mediate upon when you feel the need.

Enjoy!

Much Love,

Taya

Acknowledgements

I am grateful for all my life experiences that have brought me to this point. Each person who has come into my life has left an impression on me that can be found in these poems.

I feel blessed to have so many supports on my journey! My mother, Bridget, and my sister, Veronica, have been my biggest fans for as long as I can remember. My son, Shayne, has cheered me on through many a poetry reading with a smile that melts my heart.

I have been honored to be the messenger of these poems and have received the greatest pleasure in seeing them delivered to the souls they were intended for.

Those of you who read these poems and feel called to share them offer the biggest encouragement for me to keep writing these words that drift into my thoughts. Thank you all!

They Come Like Rain

These poems,
they fall like rain.
They come down in trickles
or torrents.
Sometimes when I least expected
and must run for cover
to record them.
It took me sometime to
see that they come like rain.
I wanted them to flow always—
like the river.
But they come by their own rhythm.
And when they are not pouring down
over me,
they are lifting up from the earth
into the clouds
and drifting towards
anyone that is ready
to catch these poems
and put them down on paper.

The Forgotten Love

We have forgotten how to love.
Real love is
not an act or gesture.
Real love is not an experience—
It is a state of being.
When we love, really love, we do not hold back.
We can't turn it off and on and off again
like a light bulb.
It just radiates
like the warmth and light of the sun.
We beam this love to everyone we meet,
not fooled by their title or what they are wearing.
If we really know how to love we
won't save it for just a few
and wrap up tight in strings of obligation.
No, if we really know how to love
with all the endless expanse of our hearts
we can't help ourselves but smile,
the smile of the master,
that even when speaking of great despair
delights in the beauty of human triumph.
The smile of the master
that opens the hearts of even the hardest warrior
and reminds them how to love.

Do Not Wait to Pray

Do not wait to Pray.
Let each breath be your prayer.
Do not wait until you are in a sacred space to pray.
Pray in the streets filled with traffic and noise
Pray in the middle of the mundane where it is least expected.
Do not wait until your hair is past your shoulders
or shaved entirely away.
Pray in the moment you wake up.
Pray just before you enter sleep
and every second in between.
When you don't know what to do—pray
and in your moments of great clarity and conviction—pray.
Let each movement become your prayer,
each gesture divine.
Let every cell in your body sing the same prayer
vibrating in the most reverent song
Let the lines blur so that prayer becomes not just
something you do,
but the state of being in which you live,
in which you love,
in which you pray.

Waterfall

You are a drop of water.
One drop.
One drop in a vast infinite flow.
Can you be both at once?
The drop and the flow—
The particle and the wave?
Yes,
you can,
but you must unlearn
that the drop is insignificant
and you must unlearn that the flow
is unloving and relentless.
When you can become both at once
you can master any terrain in which you are flowing
with the gentleness, grace and power of a river.
Even when that river plummets into the depth
it creates the beauty of a waterfall.
And as you become the river you feel the pull
of your true calling.
And when you follow your calling
The Universe follows along.

Suffering

We are here to suffer.
These words sound so negative
but sit with this.
The Buddha said all life is suffering
and some recoiled at the thought.
But look at life's design
suffering is built right in.
Yet we try so hard to avoid it
at all costs.
We don't want to be too cold,
too hot, too full or too hungry.
We are constantly striving for the balance point between two opposites.
Once one scale is balanced another one tips.
It is a maddening game.
Even our efforts to prevent suffering
cause suffering.
And yet our suffering,
it purifies us.
It cleanses away illusion
and opens us to a truth within us
that is far beyond anything we could have
experienced without it.
We are here to suffer,
not to be numb, not to move without soul through the pain
and delights of this world.
When we remember that we are here to suffer,
then we can be in a state of true happiness.

Karma

I wish to know the great patterns of Karma
To see the paths that wind us together
or pull us apart
and how very perfect this weaving is.
So much so that there is no need to resist it
but rather to skate upon it.
Gliding across it with grace
but with a sensitivity to listen
for the crack that warns
when you are about to fall in
to the icy cold waters below.
I wish I could see the backstory
behind each connection so I could better
accept the outcomes of all situations.
I wish that I could open my perspective
to see the vast timeline of this Universe expanded
so that we all become just particles
popping in and out of existence.
Then I might be able to know what the wise ones know
and not get caught up in the drama of this world.
Remembering that it is ice that I skate upon
but knowing the patterns that prevent me from falling in.

The Poems of Desire

One day
I will ask you
to read me the poems of Pablo Neruda
as if you wrote them for me.
I will ask,
because how would you ever know of this
desire without my request.
Some poets know exactly what they wanted
but were unable to ask
due to obstacles beyond their control.
And this created such delirious longing
and such spectacular poetry!
Some poets knew how to ask and what for
and held nothing back in their list of who
and what they desired
and held back nothing in their descriptions.
This too made for spectacular poetry!
I ask you to read me the love poems
of Pablo Neruda.
Next I will ask you to create poetry
with me.

Let Me Remember

"Oh please let me remember this"
I say as a poem storms through me
and captures my attention
in one of those moments where I cannot drop
everything to record it.
"Please let me remember each moment"
I think as this poem soon reminds me
of this life,
and how fleeting and ephemeral it is.
If I lose focus for one moment
how many poems of my life have I lost?
And if I don't read each word
with deep conviction and attention
then what is the point?
I didn't come here for a bland existence
not worthy of capturing.
I didn't come here not to pine
and pain and fly and crash
and rave and dance
and be perfectly still
all in the same moment.

Beauty

Do not apologize for your beauty,
if you are not finding it yet celebrated
by this world.
Your form is the perfect expression
of your Soul,
which is the perfect expression
of the Creator.
The fools who do not see the beauty in you
are missing the beauty reflected in their mirror
each morning.
Do not apologize for your beauty,
it is a gift to all who are wise enough
to receive it.

Proof

I asked the divine
How do I show them my love for you is true?
The reply came quickly
If you stop asking for proof, so will they

Appreciation

I fill the basin
with the hot, clear water.
Stopping its flow for a moment
in time
so I can sink into it.
The warmth of the water covers me
and I am safe and warm
just like before I was born
into this world.
The salt mixed into mimic the ocean,
the mother ocean,
the water of tears,
the water inside.
I bathe in it,
receiving the nourishment
it offers as it pauses on its journey.
I feel such appreciation for these
waters
that flowed into my home
and will just as easily flow out.
Realizing that if I had to carry this water,
heat this water,
this bath would never have happened.
I feel a sense of awe at the wonder of it all
and a sense of respect
for this water that I honor as it flows to me
and will flow away.
I have a deep respect for those who must work hard
for their water and let not a drop go wasted.
I have a deep respect for those who work to make
clean water flow to those in need,

since we are all in need.
I appreciate those who honor the spirit
of water as more than just a resource
but a spirit, an energy,
a living entity
that unites all the life on this planet
in its flow.

Soften

The Universe is teaching you to become soft.

Our instinct tells us
that we should be hard
to protect ourselves from pain.

Yet our shell can crack with the blows
of all that is hurled at us,
the unkind word,
the lost love,
the violence.
The crack of our shell cuts deeper
then any other weapon could.

Our instinct tells us to grow hard,
but the Universe is asking us to grow soft.

Soft, softer, softening to the flow of water.
The hard dried earth cannot take it in—
the water just flows off the surface
until the earth softens to receive it.

The warriors who can merge with the flow,
who can soften,
cannot be found by their opponent
yet the armored knight is a target for attack.

When soft the blows can pass through us,
there is no ego to resist so there is nothing to injure.
Become soft like this. Like a babe of the Universe.

Here I Am Again

Here I am again,
in the same seat as before—
the one I said I wouldn't
sit in anymore
and yet
here I am,
again.

So tired of this
crashing and burning
this falling back to where I started.
What of all the progress
I thought I was making?

I sit in this seat—
this hot seat—
as I burn myself with
insults which only add to my time
sitting in this place.

Finally I rise up,
and notice how much easier
it is to get out of the chair,
now that I have had so much practice.

Incense

The air is thick
with the incense of our prayers.
Each stick lit with an intention,
a call,
a vibration,
sent out from the heart
to the Universe
and back again.
The fragrance of spices, herbs, blossoms and woods,
gathered from far reaches,
ground together by hand with prayers recited over them.
Each stage its own blessing.
And here
I add my stick of incense
to the altar
and send my heart's prayer
across the Universe and back.

Angel

There is an angel hiding
in each person you meet.

You never know who will let
their angel awaken to you,
but they will
when you need it most.
And they will offer you a gesture
so simple
and so profound.
Their benevolence will be the piece
that was missing on your mission.

Please feel what a gift it is
when wings spread inside their heart
and they expand to be of service in this world.
Then let the wings inside your own heart expand
so that you can offer the missing piece of someone
else's great mission.

Angels & Demons

The Only way to be an Angel
is to know your Demons.

If you do not know your demons,
own your demons,
control your demons
so they respond to you
the way a dog does its master,
then your demons will pin your wings
when you least expect it.
If you pretend those demons of yours
are not there sitting right next to you
stoking the fires of your desires,
or walking you through circles
again and again,
then you will always be ruled by them.
If you want to be an angel in this world
you must know your demons, you must rule your demons.
And then you can step beyond the battle of angels and demons
and know the mind of creation.

Trust

Trust yourself,
your clear, clean, quiet self.
Trust that you know
exactly what is best
and sit back and let it come to you.
Don't talk yourself
into something that doesn't fit.
If you have to talk yourself into something,
you are going to have to back yourself out of it.

So save yourself
the time and energy
by trusting that you know.
And trusting that the Universe knows this too
and has just what you need
placed in the hands of your own soul.

Hide & Seek

After years
and years
of playing
this game of hide and seek
have you realized
that the one doing the counting
and the one hiding
are one and the same?
There is nothing to find—
other than yourself
and there is no one hiding—
other than yourself.
With this realization
you can keep playing the game,
or you can sit down
under the tree you have been counting against
and hiding behind
and just be.

Bless Them

The stores are filled
with books
on how to relate to one another,
how to relate to ourselves.
I have read my share
believe me,
but what the masters say
it is true.
Whether you love someone,
hate someone
or feel nothing for someone,
Bless them.
Bless them
no matter what.
Bless them when you most resist it.
Bless them with no strings attached.
It is far more effective
and far less complicated
than reading all the books.

Sinners & Saints

Why do you pretend you are a sinner—

When underneath it all you are a saint?

Why do you dress like a beggar—
when you are kings and queens?
Don't let the world trick you into thinking
you are less than.
Don't let anyone else determine your worth.
We all have value beyond measure.
Each being so precious
with the existence it has been given.
And since you are a saint—
act like one.
And since you are royalty—
carry yourself with the prestige of your position.
For you, my dear, are a child of God.

Nature

Even in the city
so full of humans
and their buildings.
Even under the pavement
and cement.
Nature strives to bring its beauty
to us.
The fields between the highways,
the cracks in the parking lot,
the vacant
abandoned spaces
are filled
with life and love.
Nature reserves its beauty
for nothing.
It releases it all regardless
of the witness.
It waits for no audience
or applause,
yet the wise notice.
The wise stop to witness
and then complete the circle.

Sit

I am sitting
for just a moment.
It seems that every time I pause
a poem comes through.
As though inspiration is
just waiting for a moment like this—
to shine.
Each pause a door that something
greater can come into this world.
A little glimpse of infinity
when we can become still enough
to open to it.

Gold

There was a sweetness
when we met
that spoke of a deeper sweetness
that was eager to be explored.
A vein of gold
just below the surface.
So hidden
in plain sight.
That it was hard to believe
it was real.
The sweetness continues as
we continue to explore one another—
hands across skin,
so new yet familiar.
Our words and our mouths so complimentary
when they meet.
Our bodies such a perfect fit
to hold one another.
So much love
just flowing between
our two hearts.
All this after such a time of drought.
Let the sky open up
to mirror this taste of Heaven on Earth.
Let the waters unearth
the deeper gold.
Riches beyond measure.

Courage

There is a difference in new love
that comes to us after having experienced
heartbreak.
One is hesitant and cautious
where one was previously carefree.
One is bound by the ties of the past with others
and must choose to lovingly
cut through those ties
in order to love once more.
So many hearts are held
with the words of old love lost
that new love must be patient,
kind and determined
in order to last.
Where once there were no obstacles,
now there is a draw bridge
that will only be let down for the purest and
bravest of hearts.

Sound

The voices in the darkness
are reading you poetry.
The hum of machines
are vibrating mantras.
The chatter of your thoughts
is pointing you to the silence
upon which all this rests.
All the noise of this creation
is just singing you back
to yourself.
To the moment of the first sound
where this all began.

Diamond Eye

There is a clarity in you.
A sweet quiet in your voice.
A peace in the space around you.
Your eyes so clear,
like diamonds,
reflecting the clarity
of mind.

Union

There is no I
in Yoga.
The I must dissolve
completely
and then re-emerge
in UnIon.
Then there is no one
"doing" yoga,
there is just the bliss
of unwrapping
the packages—
the one that we thought
we were,
and the one that we thought
"It" was.
As we get closer and closer
to unwrapping
this present—
we pull the layers
off faster and faster
just like the biggest
present at the birthday party
for this truly is
the moment of our birth—
where the I
is born again in UnIon.

Relax

"Relax. I have got you".
The Universe has been telling me
over and over.
"Relax and lean into me
I have got you".
Slowly these words penetrate
into me and I feel trust melting away
the fear.
I remember encouraging my child
to relax into the waters
his body able to float
and my hands beneath him
to catch him if needed.
"Relax. I have got you"
I said reassuringly
knowing that all that was needed
was for him to surrender his back to the surface,
his trust that the water would hold him
and that his own breath would keep him afloat.
Now it is my turn
to make this surrender
knowing my struggles are so futile
when all I need to do is
lay back
and relax.

Flawed Design

The flaw in my design
is that I still think of you
even though you have gone.
My hand still reaches for yours
but you are not here
and you haven't been
for many months.
Yet still
this silly flaw
makes me long for you—
though you have no longing for me.
Each day
you come into my thoughts
in the most innocent of ways,
but it is only a ghost
and old memory
that floats around me
waiting to catch me
up in its delusion.
It knows just the way
to get past the guard
I have now posted at my heart.
It knows how to get through
the maze I have put around
myself so that I can be as alone as I feel.
No one besides your ghost
can visit me here,
and so I must wait
for this apparition of what I thought
was love to grow tired of this game
and leave me in peace.

Madness

Please don't let this madness
wash over you like
a wave.
It is a wave
and it will recede
and it will wash
over you again and again.
That is the nature of
this maya.
And so we must learn
to ride the waves,
to know the ocean
the tides,
the currents.
We must know
our minds
and how to master
our own thinking
if we wish to escape
the control of others.
We must see beyond
our own pain, our own confusion
and our own fear
and see the collective suffering.
Then we must pull each other
out of the tumbling surf
and make sure everyone is safe,
and honored
and loved.
With no one
held higher than any other.

Snow

the day that the whole Universe
became light
in my awareness
was the day I understood maya.
This seemingly solid reality
became like pure white snow
that I could mold and shape
however best to suit my needs.
The world became a blank field
without footprints
for me to carve out
the creations that I wanted to share
with this reality
and to gently knock down
the structures of snow
that no longer suited my fancy.
Awash with a sense of play
that I hadn't felt
since a child
playing in the snow
without fear
holding me back from participating.

The Saints Do It Too

The Saints do it too.

All the things you are beating yourself up about,
the Saints do it too.
They thought about past lovers,
they daydreamed,
they got angry,
felt sad,
lost everything,
had nothing.

The Saints did it too.
The only difference is that
they knew that it was all God's play.
That simple reminder
can change everything.

Bonsai

To live your life well
You must treat it like a bonsai.
You must set aside the time and focus
To get into the flow,
The space of knowing.
Then you gently,
Slowly,
Trim away
Anything that is not needed.
Once the shape is perfect,
Because your heart tells you so,
You step back
And with admiration
Breathe into the beauty
You co-created,
Filling it with Prana.
Breathing life into the
Structure you have created
As a reminder of your natural way of being.

Sing

While you are here,
sing as much as you can.
No matter who is listening
or how you sound.
Just sing your song
into this world of sound.
Sing from your soul
and let the sound of your own
voice heal you.
Let the vibration of your
soul's song
heal this world.

Ward of the Universe

Try this with me.
Become a Ward of the Universe.
Try it for a short time,
like this lifetime
for instance.
Surrender your fears,
your needs,
your illusion of control,
and be completely
taken care of
by that which created you.
Let your soft bed
be made of moss
or fine feathers if that suits you.
Let your bowl be filled
with whatever is being offered
and let that nourish you deeply.
Let the Universe dress you in the costume
that serves your role in this play
that we are in.
And feel with deep confidence
that you know all your lines
by heart.
The Universe is the best director
so surrender in trust
to its leadership and care.

Mara

Don't let Mara
stop you
from carrying your search
for enlightenment
to the very end.
Mara exists just
to test your mettle.
He is made of terror
and desire
and ignorance
that has no grounds.
He is not real
there is nothing
in Mara to resist.
He comes at us strong
when we are strong
and closest to breaking through
the gate to our true happiness.
Don't stop when Mara
approaches
but with the gentlest force
shatter the gate.
It too
does not exist.

Heaven. Hell

It is all right here,
Heaven. Hell.
There is no need to wait
until death
to experience them.
They live as neighbors.
You can see them in the cars
on the freeway.
Heaven. Hell or
the dull numb that drones
through the days.
Your judgement is not withheld
until your body passes.
Its waiting for you in the next moment.
It is visible in your walk,
your talk,
your dreams—waking and not.
You live in Heaven, Hell.
Again and again
until you realize
you have a choice as to which one
you accept for your truth in this moment.

Forgetful

For a short time
I forgot myself
Completely
In you.
There was something
So familiar
That I thought
That we were one.
That some special connection
Bound me to you
Unlike any other.
I forgot that
In my true heart
There is no difference
Between you
And me
And all other beings.
In that forgetting
A great pain was felt
When you left.
But in this remembering
A deep and quiet bliss
Fills my heart
Since there is now
so much more to love.

Lover

I will teach you
The secret of how
To be the best lover.
There are no positions to memorize,
No costumes to wear,
No objects to acquire.
To be the best lover
You must love.
Love the person in front of you
With your whole heart
As the doorway through which
The infinite can flow.
And see how the infinite shines through them
See the light in their eyes,
The glow of their skin.
Feel the warmth inside them
Bursting to touch you.
Take your time in seeing them
All of them
Each cell of their being
Each fiber of energy
Until you see
How they connect to you before
You even touch.
There is no finer way to be a lover
Than this.

The Order of Things

There are moments
in which the whole universe
collapses into one point,
crushing everything together,
creating more heat and friction,
and gravity and pain
than you can fathom.
And then in the next moment,
everything turns
inside-out
and a whole new Universe is born
and begins spinning in an orderly fashion.

Now is one of those moments.
Experiencing
this dance of sound and fury,
waiting with slow breath,
until everything falls back
into natural order.

Here

I am right here.
Even in this moment
Where you feel like you
Have fallen away from me.
Even in this moment where
Your drunken gaze makes it hard for you to feel me,
I am here.
Don't let yourself believe
You have wandered too far away,
That you are beyond my reach,
I am here.
And I watch you lovingly,
Without judgment as you
Navigate the wall that you are climbing.
It doesn't matter to me whether you climb up or down.
I am here.
Here to witness your progress,
Here to acknowledge your effort,
Right next to you.
And if you fall,
I fall as well
Yet I trust that you will
Rise to the challenge,
As you will,
And that you will recall my promise to never leave you.
And you will trust in me as I in you
And make your great journey together

Little Moon

Oh moon that I am.
Always reflecting
whatever light comes to me,
but not able to create my own.
Trying so hard
to draw to me
something magnificent
when I am
so small and
so easily overlooked.
Little orb
of rock and dust
so desolate as I spin
locked on one
who is not locked on me.
Little moon
who longs to be the Sun.
Yet is left with just reflecting
the light I can catch and release.
Not knowing
the pull
that my longing has
on the oceans beneath me,
or the madness my full light creates.
The volumes of
poems and songs
all written
about this moon's
desire to reflect
her beloved.

The Mirror

There is a mirror
that will show you the inner workings
of the Universe.
A smooth surface
like the waters of a still pond
that can reflect
the brilliance of the Cosmos
when quiet,
or the chaos of distortion
when rippled.
This mirror can bring
to the light
your own depths,
the roots of each thought and action—
the real source of your being.

There is a screen on which
your whole life is projected,
You—the director, producer and starring lead.
The projector itself lies inside you
beaming from the center of your mind.

You can watch the same film
again and again,
or open yourself to a new experience.
The choice is yours—each moment.
The screen, the mirror, surround you,
but they are not fixed.
To gaze into this mirror
all you need to do
is open up all of your eyes.

Study this mirror and know it as yourself,
For now,
for one day both the screen and the mirror
will fall away completely
and you will understand what you truly are.

Your Rhythm

Do the work,
take the stumble
and learn this
dance that is being presented.
At first there is no music
but then you feel your way.
Then your feet begin
to find their confidence
as they lift from the earth.
Your body finds
its own rhythm
and the whisper of
your song
can be heard.
Then,
slowly,
another joins you.
You find your way
to dance together.
Their dance may fit
with yours
and you may wish to dance with them forever.
It may not,
and you may thank each other
and move on.
The only rule is that you keep
dancing.
Resting only when needed
and stepping back into your rhythm
altering yourself as your connection
to the music grows.

Worthy of Love

There was a moment
that hurt so deep
it made you think
you were not
worthy of love.
The thought was so
painful, so frightening
that a wave of numbness
flooded over you
In that moment you had two paths—
to throw the thought away as ridiculous,
or to accept the thought and let it resurface
whenever you didn't handle yourself with care.
Those who let the thought have their way
have the vigorous task of clearing the field
that has been planted year after year
with the seeds of agony and self loathing.
The task must be done so that their field
doesn't spread to neighbors or future generations.
The task must be done so that they can
realize the truth—
that every being,
in every moment,
is worthy of love,
no mater what.

Summer

this heat
this fire
is burning away
with ease
all that no longer serves.
This heat
keeps my anger on a
high simmer
ready to roll at the first
sign of feathers ruffling.
"It is Summer"
I remind myself each time
I feel the heat rising.
It is Summer
and I seek to dive into
the heat to purify my being
and then dive into the cool
to temper my steel.

Please Show Me

Show me your soul.
I want to see all the way
down to the bones of your being—
the structure that makes
you stand like you do.
Then I want to gaze
deeper into you,
so deep,
that I can see the
fibers that weave you
together in the shroud
of your body.
And I am not going to
stop there.
I want to see further
into the very vibration
of your sound
of your true being
of your soul.
I want to disrobe
all of my layers to meet
you in this place of
pure energy,
pure ecstasy.
I am not afraid
of the pain
and confusion
that could come from
an encounter like this.
Because in reality
this is all that there is.

Limitless Supply

Why do you hide from this Love?
Do you think what is being delivered
was given to you by mistake?
Do you think you are not ready,
worthy, holy, dirty
enough to receive me?
Do you think there is a hidden price tag,
a catch,
a trade off
that would be made from taking this love?
Do you not see the burden
that is created when the flow
of love is denied?
I say this only because
I can see how much you want this love.
I can see the fear in your eyes
and hear the resignation in your voice
as you try to turn away from it.
"Here,"
I say,
as I put your hand on my heart,
"There is a limitless supply.
Let what is yours flow to you.
And open yourself to love."

Woman

The only mystery of woman
is that she is a complete, unsolvable mystery.
One you could never understand
for woman has not been
encouraged to know herself
and even the knowing is only
a pointing towards
the dynamic play
that is Woman.

The mind will never be able to capture
the essence of woman,
so let go of the mind.
The heart is the place to go.

Love a woman like you would love a wild thing.
A lioness who has separated from her pride
and in her curiosity allows you to come near.

Feel your awe for her,
but do not be surprised if beckons you
as a lover and then stalks
you as her prey.
It is not her fault
she is trying to make sense of it
as much as you.

When you see one woman
you see the facets of generations of women,
you see the faces of the thousands
of goddesses this world

has tried to box in,
naming one harlot,
one virgin, one healer, one wise one, one warrior—
forgetting that each woman,
each goddess is all of these
to meet the moment
to rise to the occasion.

The Chase

The mind wants so badly
to understand
this mystery.
Each person on your path
holds a clue.
Each quiet moment
offers the chance of insight.
The mind tries
to weave them together
in some form
that make sense to it, but
this world
is not meant
for sense
and understanding.
This world is meant
for wonder and awe.
As soon as the mind
picks up the trail—
the Universe changes
course or climbs
up and out of reach, but
as soon
as you sit still and open
your heart with each breath,
the Universe
can no longer resist you
and surrounds
you with its infinite embrace.

Hidden Things

It is the Hidden Things
that I would love about you
if you would show them to me.
I have my Hidden Things too.
For years I have been slowly
bringing them out into the open softly
like hands full of sand.
Sifting through myself
to find the treasure and the trash
that I had buried.
The Hidden Things that
change the way my life flowed.
Just like the Hidden Rocks
on the beach
change the course
of each wave.
I want to show you
my Hidden Things
without labeling them
Treasure or Trash.
You may have a use for what
I would discard and no interest
in what I treasure,
but the Hidden can no longer
remain so in my Heart.
Let us lay down this blanket
and show the Hidden Things
we have been too scared to share with others.
For here there is only Love.

The Cavern

When the Earth opens up
and slowly pulls you in,
you can go willingly
into the depression,
even though you are scared.
The pull will not go away
but will only act as an anchor
that will slow you down,
as you press on
trying not to alter your course,
until you are buried to your knees
in earth.
When the Earth opens
up to pull you into
the depression
know that it is
a whole new realm of
mystery that lies
within yourself,
Stop everything.

Let yourself rest
into the warm arms of the Mother.
Let the deep sleep
come over your mind
so that your soul
can speak clearly to your heart.
Let your heart be filled
with the instructions it will
need to carry you through the next journey.
Let your mind and ego be reworked

into new devices to assist you in your travels.
Let your body melt into its natural state
so that it can rise up with the comfort
and freedom of youth.
Do not run from the depression
the Earth has carved out for you.
It is only through the caverns
deep within the Earth
that we can see the reaches
of the sky.

Good Day

When I say "have a good day"
I am saying
I hope this day makes you feel alive.
I hope something that no longer serves you falls away.
I hope something shocks you awake and reminds you of what really matters.
I hope you experience a little pain, a lot of wonder, moments of being lost, moments of being found, and moments of contented stillness in between.
And when you go to sleep tonight
I hope you feel like you are one step closer to your truth.

Diamonds

You are a shining stone
embedded in the sooty darkness.
The outside will not reflect back your light
but absorb it.
Don't let that stop you
from reflecting out your light.
Know that your light
penetrates even the immense darkness
which is not an empty witness
to your soul.

We say it is the pressure that turns
the coal to diamond.
But it could also be said
it is the diamond's desire for light
that creates the pressure
to transform.

Waiting Room

I made a promise
to myself.

To wait.
To wait
until that clear
YES
comes before moving forward.
I promised to
put my comfort
before their wants
and to put my bar
out of reach.
Only if
someone will take
the time,
the creativity,
the dedication
and the love
required to not only find
but reach that bar
will they be invited in,
in to the waiting room.
Where they too can make
a promise to themselves
to wait
until they know that clear
YES
before we take hands
and move on.

Your True Name

I saw you as you are.
In that moment
I tattooed your true name
Upon my heart.
Knowing the ache
It would leave behind
If you were to go
But knowing no other way
To love you
I let Love emboss me
With your presence.
No matter where life
Takes you,
You will always have a home
In the vastness of my heart.

Humans

The beauty of us humans,
Is that we are so very human.
So filled with light
And so full of shadow.
So many tools at our disposal
These forms, this mind, this heart.
We can take the earth
And lift it up to the heavens
And we can draw the heavens
Down to touch the sweet earth.
Like a bridge in every direction.
We are sometimes so clear in our purpose
And sometimes so lost without hope
But we are always a gateway to the entire universe.

Open

This urge to close down
Is overtaking me.
I feel the strength of the wind building
And tossing me without remorse.
Like an umbrella in the storm
I could close down to keep safe
To find shelter.
But it is too late for closing down.
That has never been an option.
Since I cannot close
I must open fully to the storm.
So open that I turn myself inside out
Until there is nothing hidden
Nothing defended
Just the wind
The breath of life
Flowing through me
Ripping apart anything
That is closed
And locked
And forgotten.
Breaking away the past ways that are of no use
And elevating the true ways
That want to live again in this world.
That want to teach us how to love
With hearts blown open
And minds that know their
way to the Beloved.

Our Storm

I need someone who can handle
the weight of my heart,
the depth of my feelings,
the vastness of my love.
Not everyone could handle
this storm of energy heading their way.
Some will run at the first sign,
some will stand strong
until the winds stir them too much.
But one will have feet solid in the Earth
and a head held in the Heavens
and a storm as powerful as mine
that dances in the opposite direction.
And when those two storms meet
there will be a stillness neither of us have ever shared before.
Time will stop with the storms howling
and the golden light will pour through this moment
and will last as long as We do.

Huntress

I concealed my weapons
and moved silently
through the world.
Tracking the creatures
I thought were meant for me.
And being tracked
by other's doing the same.
Some trails were lost
and picked up again.
Some ended as soon as they began,
others lingered and then left
abruptly.
My senses warned me of all of this,
but my hopeful heart had to see
each hunt through to the end.
There was no prize from this practice
beyond learning so
I have stopped my tracking
stopped hunting,
and instead stand—
like a living statue—

and wait for the one
who has been seeking me—
always a few steps behind me in the shadows.
Waiting until I am done with my playing
and ready to begin again.

Truth

The truth will not hurt you
if you see the gifts that it holds.
This is wisdom,
understanding,
expansion,
clarity.
In exchange you must
hand over
fear, insecurity,
suffering,
loneliness.
Your ego is the only thing
that takes a hit
when the truth comes,
but all the real facets of
yourself expand into their natural state.

The Reconcile

You set everything down
and I did the same.
We matched as much of what we held
as we could
until all that remained
were the differences between us.
The differences that kept us
worlds apart.
We realized that we were not a match
for the other
and a gentle tear fell.
We pressed our hearts together once more
and released the desire
for more than just this moment of sweetness together.
I placed my things in my basket
and you drew the blanket around all that you shared.
I smiled as I turned
and you did the same.
Parting ways slowly
with love in our hearts
and the hope for the next match to appear.

Wither

I am not going to collapse
in despair,
not going to wither away
like a fallen leaf.
Just because he is leaving me.
This isn't the first time.
I have survived
more shocking separations
and it is not without my approval
that he is going.
I know there will be moments
when memories pull me to a past
that is no longer relevant,
a taste of hopes I thought would become.
There will be tears
and the dance of shaking him off,
but because of this a new understanding
of me will emerge
and I will explore this new self
like a snake with fresh skin.
I will feel things I have missed
and sense a new language with the world.
The only thing that will wither
is an old form that I used to call "me"
and without that I
can glow.

Special Someone

I love that breath
that gets caught
just above your heart
when you see
the one with that special
something.
Their gravity
slows time.
Their presence
unlocks a secret magic
that was hiding behind
everything.
Even your own body
switches itself
into a whole new way
of being.
The heart beats faster,
the skin softens and blooms
blood reaching,
the eyes open wider
drawing in ever detail,
the mind becomes so
aware.
Locking each experience to memory
to remember the moment
the Special Someone first appeared.

Dark

Do not worry.
Your eyes will adjust to the darkness
and you will see the light that is there.
Your mind will expand its bounds
when it can no longer rely on the eyes for containment.
And once vision is surrendered
it will return again
with more clarity and sensitivity
as if you have never seen before
giving you a wonder for all that is put before you.

Moth

How many moths
Regret being lost to the flame?
They are drawn to the candle
lit upon my altar.
I watch them
in my meditation
as they are pulled in by the light.

They dive for it with such
boldness.
As if the fear of perishing
was never in their thoughts.
Could I be that brave?
To go beyond letting go
to the point where no thought
holds me back
from diving into the fire.
No hesitation
when the Divine flame
appears to me.
I will not know if I will
let fear overcome the urge
to be extinguished in the light.
But I hope in that moment
to be as brave as the moth
and leave nothing behind.

Shadow King

You are my Shadow King
and I wanted you to love me.
I tried to follow you each time
you left
Disappearing into the Shadow.
I found you again and again
in the eyes of others.
Yet each time the dance was the same,
recognizing you,
holding you,
then releasing or being released
when the song was done.
The longing or loathing
that filled the space in between
our visits.
The pain of apparent separation
so all encompassing yet irresistible.
The rest of the world just an interruption
of the drama between me and my Shadow King.

Until I realized the Shadow King
was a piece of me—
a borrowed shroud that I would hang between
me and my lovers.
Through which I could see what I wanted and
let the rest remain hidden
until the day the veil was lifted
and the Shadow King disappeared.

The search continued again and again
ending in this moment
when I hold the shroud in my hands.
I hold the Shadow King as my own at last.
Winning the game by forfeit.
I will no longer chase what is already mine.

Terma

Show me the real.
Show me the true.
I ache for something solid
to rest my feet upon.
I ache for something
of substance to sink my teeth into.
So many years on this diet of empty.
Feed me something real!
Something from the Earth,
untampered, unaltered,
untainted by the forgeries of man.
Teach me something real!
Too long I have tried to memorize what is untrue
and recite it back to them
as if my repeating would fill the void
of their "truths."
I want to know truths beyond
what has been shared with me
I want to dig deep into the Earth
for her mysteries to teach me
what the mind of man cannot.
And when these treasures are unearthed
I will bring them to you
to nourish you too
and fill you with the deep knowing
of what is true.

Man

I want to walk next to you,
matching my smooth stride to yours.
I want to extend myself fully
to rise to your strengths
so that they become my own.
I want to be the gentle hand that
guides you through the places
you do not yet know.
There are moments I want to be so soft
with you so that you can melt with me
and there are moments
I want to be stronger than I have know
myself to be standing solidly in the foundation
you are offering me.
I want to learn from you the ways of being
a man, so I can honor your world.
I want to show you my ways of being woman
so you can see my world as well.
I want to reach out and touch you from a place
of deep knowing so that when we come together
we are two worlds in harmony
and when we move separately we reverberate
each other's song out of reverence and respect.

Study

I used to be a scholar,
studying the Religions of the World.
But the teachings had unexpected
effects on me,
and soon my mind lost interest in cataloging
the details of the Divine
and wanted to dive inside of it
and lose myself and my mind
in the experience beyond.
Instead of knowing facts
I wanted to let go of everything
I had learned and sit down at the feet
of the nameless guru inside of me.
I threw my studies aside in exchange for living
and breathing the fragrance of heavens.
I have no regrets for my change in studies!

Love Unfulfilled

There is no such thing as love unfulfilled
The universe said to me when I demanded
Why the love I had been looking for was found
But never made it to fruition.
There is only love.
The love experienced
The love that changed shape
And remains even after the story has changed.
There is not love unfulfilled.
I sit with this in denial
Saying but…,
Until I realize it is true.
There is only love.
I sit on the shore as the waves gently reach towards me.
The stones so smooth and cool beneath the heat inside me.
You made all of this for me.
I realize
Appreciating each detail.
Thank you I say to the benevolent force behind the thought,
the creation and execution of this design.
And the love I thought yet unmanifested comes to me
Like the wave and gently
overwhelmed me with simple bliss that
hasn't left me since.

Old Love

What makes you think you must pack up
Old Love into a box and be done with it?
What makes you think you have to clean up
Old Love like it was a disaster, a mistake
that wasn't meant to be?

Old Love is meant to be mixed into the earth to make good soil.

Old Love is meant to be threaded like prisms on a strand to hang on the window so that the light shines through it and casts beams this way and that.

Old Love is meant to be made into a mosaic with pieces from what worked and pieces of what didn't that you piece together to make a stepping stone that will guide you in the direction of what will work.

Don't throw away Old Love, don't hide the feelings you have for Old Loves.

Honor them, elevate them and let that Old Love be a fuel that will ignite New Love instead of smothering the flames.

For there truly is no Old Love or New Love, it is all One Love.

Remember Me

There was a light of recognition
that flickered through my heart
when you appeared
so subtly.
Thinking it imagined
I let it slip away…
but it simmered inside me
waiting for the moment
where we both
were awakened to the energy
between us.
Energy that was tangible
even from great distances.
I could suddenly feel you beside me
in such a familiar way it was me magnified.
Through this connection our hearts both
expanded to fill the space between us.
Reaching us to our limits
as all love should.
I nourish this connection with each breath.
Not knowing what will come of this,
but knowing love is never wasted.
So even as my mind cries out
my heart knows that there is only love.

Sister | Brother

You are my sister
though I don't know you.
You and I look nothing alike
or we could be twins
it doesn't matter to me
as we are sisters.
There is no need to compete
cause we are playing this game of life
together.
You know this
or maybe you are learning
but we are remembering that it is not
the game that we were given
that we are here to play.
We set down the old ways
and the tools forced in our hands
and walk away from the manicured field
to the wild open grasses
and take hands as we run through the
unknown and familiar.

You are my brother
though we have not met
and we are dressed in different shapes and guises.
We are alike in so many ways
and different in just as many
but our differences are strengths
not weaknesses.
We too remember that it is not a battle
between us

but a playful curiosity in this adventure we
are on.
When we meet each other in a place
of love and respect
we discover there is so much for us to learn
from each other.
You are my brother
a warrior, a Sun for the Moon,
and as we set down the script that has been
handed down from our recent ancestors
we remember this world is our stage
and Brothers and Sisters,
Friends and Lovers
all take this moment to shake free
from old structures
and come alive to our connections.

One

One Breath connects us All.
One Pulse unites the rhythm of this Planet.
One Dance pulls each star in its Embrace.
Release any illusion that you are separate, alone.
Dive into the river that races through you.
Touch your hands to your Heart,
and then reach them out to Serve.

Wick

After so many years of meditation,
candle illuminating my altar,
I realized that all that I "know" as me
is merely a wick.
My body, my mind, just the wick.
My soul is the heat and light
of this candle that I am.
There could be no light without a good wick.
So I draw myself up tall
as I sit on my cushion
so that as a wick
I will produce
the most radiant light
I can.

Elements

When was the last time you honored the
Elements that you use each day?
The Earth that built your form.
The Fire that cooks your food
and warms you.
The Water that washes you,
inside and out.
The Air that fills and moves
through the empty Space
within you.
When was the last time you sung
to the Waters?
Danced for the Fires?
Blessed the Earth
with your bare feet?
Nature is calling you out.
Calling you to the wildness
where the Elements
are not contained
by human hands.
Reminding you that the Elements
that make up everything in the Universe
are inside of you.
When was the last time you honored
yourself as a Divine Dance of the Elements?

Dream

What do you do when the one you love
sleeping next to you is suffering
in their dreams?
You may desire to wake them quickly
so their struggle will end
but you could also wrap your arms
around them,
soothe them with your words,
and let them sleep just long enough
to resolve the struggle of the dreams
and then gently wake them to another reality.
That same approach that works so good at night
also works well when our eyes are open
during the day.

Close

Close is not close enough.
Like a cat,
I had tried to fit myself
into whatever container
was needed for
this connection to work.
It was so much work
to hold myself in just
the right way
or talk myself again and again
into making this work.
Yet, close is not close enough.
There is one who will not require
convincing or contorting
to experience the love I want.
I am inspired to soften myself
into my natural shape
so that the one I want
will know it is me
who is waiting for them.

This World

This World
is such a precarious dance
of extremes
and oppositions.
One moment an up
another a down.
One action for peace
another for war.
The goodness
seems overwhelmed by the bad
until the scales tip once more.
Only for a brief moment
are the scales ever balanced
in stillness
until the dance resumes.
I have climbed to the scales
and tried to pull them in my favor
again and again
but it was useless.
Once I had given up
I sat next to the scales
and settled down my anger
at how unfair this process seemed to be.
When still
I noticed the scales
also became still.
The quiet in me
drew the scales into balance.
I was confused how I could influence
something as vast as the scales that measured

the weight of the good and bad in
this World.
Instead of acting against these forces
I had more pull in sitting,
shifting
myself.
With that insight I remain
sitting in front of the scales.
Breathing myself into the peace
I wish to create in this world
and finding the balance point
in between.

Naked

I am coming to you
without charms,
without veils,
without a facade
to hide behind.
Each step I take
closer to you
I am shedding a layer
so that you can see me.
All of me.
The gems of my being
with all of their flaws
turned so you can see them.
I will not hide,
burning through anything that
does not reflect my soul
so that I can be a clear mirror.
I come to you,
naked of ego,
illusion, games,
expectations.
Surrounded only by love.
I walk with bare feet
on the path between us.
Knowing that you are doing the same.

Whenever Water is Near

Set your Holy Books down
and stick your feet into these waters.
They could be the Ganges
or the fountain in the square.
It doesn't matter where you are
the Divine is there waiting for you
to stick your feet in and then
sink deep into the waters.
Let go of any idea of understanding the Infinite,
let go of the furrowed brow that is seeking answers.
Instead do what the children do
whenever water is near.
Dive in.
Let it heal you.
Let it wrap itself around you,
finding its way into you.
Just like the Divine is doing
when you welcome it.

Lost I

Let yourself be lost
even when you know where you are going.
Don't assume that you know the road ahead
even if it appears you have walked it many times.
Wander the trail
with fresh eyes and a curious nature.
Falling in love with everything you see
since it is filled with wonder
if you take the time to go beyond
the surface.
Let yourself be lost
for then your soul
can find you.

Lost II

The moments in which
I have felt completely lost,
without purpose,
without direction
even without a care,
have ended up being the moments
in which I was most present,
most receptive,
most aware
and in that way most found.
It is then that I had my feet
most firmly planted to the Earth
and my feet pointing like a compass needle
into just the right direction
for the moment when the flow and I
reconnect and it is time
to move forward.

Equinox

This moment of balance
so precariously placed
between the past and the future.
Like walking a tight rope,
we move forward into something
unknown,
with only the stars to catch us.
The past does not have a hold on us
and the future has hands wide open
full of whatever we ask from it.
Feel where you place your foot.
Breathe as you keep your balance
and instead of looking down
look straight ahead into the mystery.

Poisons

There are many poisons
In this world,
Greed, anger, ignorance,
But the most excruciating poison
I have tasted
Is resentment.
You cannot recognize its flavor
But it coats everything you swallow.
It kills your joy so slowly you don't
Know to reach for the remedy
Until lonely years have passed.
But in every moment
The antidote is near you.
In the amulet that is your heart.
It is forgiveness
And when you reach for it to give to others
You must first taste of it yourself.
That first taste can cascade through
All hurt, all anger
In you and in others
So that others do not have to drink the antidote
For the poison you took.
I am reaching for my amulet now,
Knowing that if I am sharing these words with you
There must still want some poison to remedy in me.

The Queen Upon Her Throne

I do not speak the name of my Beloved.
For one name cannot hold Him.
As soon as I try to reach for Him
He disappears
yet surrounds my every cell
in His embrace.
I cannot speak the name of my Beloved
for all sound just points to Him,
leaving Him unspoken.
I have called for Him by many names
and He honors my attempts,
but the only moments
I have ever come face to face,
eye to eye
to my Beloved
is when I honor every particle of the countless Universe
as a piece of Myself
and raise myself up into His lap
as a Queen upon her throne.
In those moments
there are no names, no words,
just everything and nothing
in their sacred dance.

A Bottle to Hold Everything

I am so full
ready to burst
with all that wants to come through.
The words I can't write fast enough,
the love that fills me until I can't breathe
and then pulls me under the deep waters
until I am gasping.
I have to open to the Infinite
to become a bottle to hold everything
and empty myself again and again
so that these waters flow through me
without getting in the way of The Way.

Channeling Love

I want to cover the places
where there were once bruises
with the softest kisses and tears
as my heart weeps for your suffering.
I want to hold your face in my hands
so that I can look right into your eyes,
your soul
and see you for all that you are.
If I can give you this moment,
everything else that follows
will be an added gift.
Nothing expected,
nothing to cling too.
Just two souls offering healing
to one another
by channeling Love.

Your Breathing

Some times I imagine
what your breathing would sound like
if we were to be intimate together.
I have been listening to you breathing
to hear the subtle language that you speak.
There is so much we share with one another
in the moments of meditation
we share.
My mind can't help but wonder
what your breath would sound like
in moments of ecstasy that we could experience together.

Ghosts

Oh the gentle phantoms that we are for each other.
Coming into focus just long enough
to grow comfortable with one another
and then just as quickly as we drew our first
breath we are gone from this world.
Such a fleeting flickering flame
that is blown out when the great wind fills
the temple hall.
My son has asked many times if I believe in ghosts.
How can I not when my own identity is ephemeral
and impermanent?
We are all ghosts in this world
yet don't be disheartened.
When you know you are a ghost you have no fear of dying
and you choose just what places you wish to haunt instead of
being powerless to your surroundings.
Come then let us walk these halls
and wake those who are sleeping with our howls
of longing for the deepest experience of Truth.

Bonfire

I am on fire—
and you stand there,
so cool,
not consumed by the flames.
How can you be so calm
when the passion is strong
between us?
It makes me ache to hold
back from the fire
and so I cast myself
deeper into the blaze—
yet I burn alone.
I am made of this fire
so I have no fear of being
destroyed by it,
and you are too.
Why won't you join me in this
fire we built together?
Are you waiting until the sparks
of this bonfire reach the stars?
Or have you decided not to partake
in the flames now that you see how hot it burns?
I wait,
this is not the first time I was set a glow
and filled with the fire
only to sit alone as the fire turned to embers
and left only ashes in their wake.
I know how to make the most of this fire,
but what I long for is someone who is not afraid
to join me in this bonfire.

Courtesan

Don't give up on the Divine
just because she doesn't come running
the first time you call out to her.
She is not a simple harlot offering her charms to any passerby.

She is a talented Courtesan
shrouded in beauty
and hidden behind the veil of everything.

One must prepare themselves with purifications
and austerities to walk the path to her garden.
Once inside the garden walls
one must bow to the stones that guide the way.
One must take in each fragrance, each blossom,
yet not take from the treasures being presented.
One must remove all attire yet clothe oneself in one's finest
in preparation to meet her gaze.

When one reaches the temple of the Goddess
be it built by the hands of man or the dance of the Goddess herself,
there is nothing left to do but wait,
wait to see how she will meet you.

There is no doubt she will greet you,
She is inside you right now and surrounds you completely.

The question is only how will you acknowledge her?
Will she hide shyly behind her screen?
Will her veiled face be visible through the window?
Will she step onto the path and meet you eye to eye?

Or will she take you down to the earth in the deep embrace of a lover?

She will do all of this, but how much of this can you perceive? The more we see Her dance in all of Creation the better a Lover we can become.
Oh, she is such a fine Courtesan. With love for all as she is all that we know.

Sky Dancer

She who is all of space
dances through me.
I have let myself become
as open to the air
as a tattered prayer flag
so that she can move in me
without impediments.
The winds are roused
as I write this,
confirming this great
Wisdom Being's
desire to dance through
the curtain of illusion
and free us from our fears.
With the biggest love in her
vast heart
she tears through each of
us in an instant
what takes the winds
years to destroy.

Melt

I want to melt into your arms—Now!
The distance between us
dissolving into the emptiness
that it is.
I want to soften in that embrace
and set aside the armor
that my mind still clings too.
I want to open into the deep bliss
that only fearless hearts
can enter.
In that Bliss I want to merge
as one,
Uniting everything.
Oh the pain from thinking I am separate
from this when you are so far from me!

I Want You

There is something
I want you to say to me.
And that is
"I want you."
I have shared time with others
who were never clear that I was
what they wanted.
By mistake, I had made myself
a convenient option and never
required these words spoken
before we slipped away unnoticed.
It wasn't until I noticed
the words were never said
that I realized the mistake was made.
Now that I am wiser
I will wait
off the beaten path
and out of view
until the one searches for me
and finds me alone
and looks me in the eyes
and says to me
"I want you."
I will sit with these words
and see how it feels to receive
them, and only if the words feel true
upon hearing and upon speaking
will I say
"I want you, too."
I want you to say these words to me,
but you must say them first
and I will wait for you to find me
and will be listening with all my heart.

Longing

I lay here in this longing
in the time between our visits.
Recreating moments together in my thoughts.
I feel the touch of your finger
weaving back and forth
from the curve of my neck
around the curve of my breast,
across my belly,
my hips,
and finally to the hidden
curve deep within me.
You explore me with such boldness
and tender familiarity
Opening me gently
pressing through the illusion
of separation.
Longing for union even as we share such a
deep embrace.

Season

Another season is passing
as I sit alone.
The cold of winter was hard
without a love to keep me warm.
Wishing to sleep away the time
instead of building a fire to enjoy.
Spring was excruciating
to be surrounded by so much beauty
with no one to share it with.
Each blossom so perfectly mirroring
what I wanted to do for the one
I was calling for each night.
Summer is now the most painful
with the hot nights that demand
naked skin on fresh sheets
this heat that makes old loves keep their distance
at night makes this lone lover toss and turn
in her anguish of longing.
Fall too will be a challenge if I must spend it on my own.
If that be the case, I will do as the trees do and let go of all
attachments and expectations.
Knowing that Nature is always offering up Her ecstasy if I can
perceive it beyond my senses and frail ego.
My heart's prayer is that the Lover is here beside me now
as I experience all of this and sharing the same exquisite
longing as we sense each other through the veil.

Smolder

I am waiting
in this heat
and this smoke.
To see if this fire
will spark.
Smoldering.
slowly,
carefully.
Like the prey
that moves softly
to call no attention.
Like the predator
that wastes no energy
on that which
does not serve
its survival.
Coiled,
resting,
waiting.
Poised to move
if needed
but hoping you
move first
and from that motion
I will find the movement
of all the stars
that brought us to this moment
and understand
if we are meant to smolder
or to ignite.

Like This

Let me show you
how I want to be touched.
How I want you to hold me.
Let me show you
the way I want to be treated
in this moment
and then tell you when this moment
changes into new desires.
Let me show you
and then you can decide if
what I am asking for is in alignment
with what you want to give.
If so, then I want you to show me
how you want to be treated
how you want to be held
and touched in this moment.
If we are lucky, we will have many
more moments together
like this.

The Soul's Poem

There is a secret poem
hidden in your heart.
You don't need to write it,
It was written the moment
you were born,
and is waiting for you to discover it.
You may have uncovered a line of it
here and there.
You may have forgotten it completely
for months and years.
It may come to you all at once
as you race to write the words down
so they will last.
But they will last
because this is the poem of your soul.
These words are more infinite
than anything else you will create in this life.
The wise ones quiet themselves each day
to go within to hear the angels sing to them
the poem of their soul.
In your quest for wisdom follow that same path
back to the soul's poem within.

Essence

I am not going to tell you
what you should be doing
or the benefits of this or that
diet, practice, teaching.
There is plenty of wisdom on how
to be happier, healthier, smarter.
All I can do is give you a taste
of the quiet wisdom beyond all of this
and hope that my words,
and the vast space
hidden between them,
will make you hunger for your own
path to the place where your true essence
lives.

If Anyone Was Watching

If anyone was watching,
they would see the way we
are slowly leaning in towards
each other.
Feeling into the space in between
us as it starts to grow
slightly smaller
with each passing breath.
They might see the energy
buzzing between us
and wonder how we can resist
diving into one another
like they do in all the movies.
If any one was watching
they may be cheering for us
to press our lips together
and find our way to the ground.
Even though no one is watching
we treat each other with utmost care
and deep respect.
Passing closely again and again
not falling into each other's orbit,
but open to that possibility if that is
in the great plan.

Thousand Steps to Spirit

It takes a thousand steps
to get to Spirit.
From the roots in the Earth
across the waters of the Ocean.
Through the fires of the Will.
The staircase is not easy to follow,
some never make it this far.
There is a quiet stretch where it feels like you are
making no progress at all.
Finding your way with your hands on the cool stone.
It can be maddening…
until a whole new world of fresh air opens up and you can
breathe again.
The staircase continues up the mountain side for another
stretch of quiet.
Each step becomes lighter but again it seems like walking in
place.
If you just keep going everything starts to open up once more
and we feel the summit is near.
As you approach you realize you have traveled farther than you
could have ever imagined. You see the climb you have made
and can't even recognize the Self that started the journey.
Then all climbing stops.
No steps remain.
Now you must sit, and soar to Spirit.
When the Soul and Spirit reunite
you see that not only did Spirit built the perfect way
home for Soul, but it guided you through every step.

Kindness

In each moment
there are a million billion
acts of kindness.
They happen so naturally
that it is easy to overlook them.
There is so much care that we
have for one another:
The mother reaching for her
child's hand as they cross the street in safety.
The wife that helps her husband from
the car to his wheelchair.
The husband that takes silly photos
to bring a smile to his dying wife's face.
The elders who just rest in love
and are available to us when we slow down with them.
There is just so much love in the world!
It is like the air we breathe.
It is like a reflex and so we don't even see
how our own love guides everything we do,
and we can miss the love that others have for us.
Train yourself to look for love
and soon it will be all that you see.

A Taste of This Love

You are going to receive
the greatest love in your life…
but it is going to come to you in
the most unexpected ways,
and when you least expect it.
It will come to you when your back
is turned to it.
It will chase you for miles and miles
as you run further from it.
It will take a shape you don't recognize,
at first.
It will come from a place where once there
was anger or hurt.
It will fill all the emptiness inside of you
and surround you with its embrace
so that you feel like you are going to burst
with gentle bliss.
Oh, Love, it is chasing you now,
surrounding you now,
waiting for you now
to just trust into its timing,
its all pervasiveness
and just enjoy each and every taste of this Love.

About the Poet

I was born near Mt. Shasta in California. As curious, intuitive child, I had a natural tendency towards spirit and poetry and a challenging time being in the world.

I found my voice in poetry and remember my mother driving us through a blizzard in the high Sierras where I grew up to get me to my first poetry reading. There I fell in love with reading poems and I also fell in love with my first lover.

In college on the North Coast in Arcata, I studied the Religions of the World focused on Eastern Traditions and the Religions of the Goddess.

That is when the name Taya came to me from the name of a Buddhist deity.

I moved to the foothills in Nevada City, California, to focus on herbalism and healing and took the name Malakian upon getting married to my son's father.

As I deepened my yoga practice and began teaching I was given the name *Gopalpreet*, which means the beloved of the Divine, much like my birth name Tiffany, appearance of the Divine.

You could say the Universe has been guiding me in circles and the poems are the songs of that journey.

I am grateful for the opportunity to share these poems with you. Enjoy both the Love and the Longing!

www.ingramcontent.com/pod-product-compliance
Lightning Source LLC
Chambersburg PA
CBHW070504100426
42743CB00010B/1749